The Pearl City Blues
A Chuck Polanski Novel

The Pearl City Blues
A Chuck Polanski Novel

Sometimes you climb out of bed in the morning and you think, I'm not going to make it, but you laugh inside – remembering all the times you've felt that way.

- Charles Bukowski

ONE

It was like any other day in my sad little life.

Up at dawn, two beers and a shot of single malt, then a long hot shower before sitting down at my computer to hopefully come up with something worth reading.

Like I said, just like any other day.

#

Or I'd thought so at the time.

As the day went on, it was much more than a tad bit eventful.

First of all, I had ended up with a case of the dreaded writer's block. Then, to make matter much worse, I'd run out of single malt.

It was time for a trip to the liquor store, post haste.

On the way there, I'd become quite thirsty, and had dropped by the neighborhood tavern for a cold beer.

Bud's tavern was normally a pleasant atmosphere.

After the owners and other patrons got used to seeing you, it was like you were a member of their family. It sort of reminded me of that old TV show, *Cheers*, where, as the title song says, "everybody knows your name."

Each time I walked in the door, there were the

same friendly faces and smiles waiting for me, as well as the obligatory ribbing and joking. Considering the fact I had recently gone through a divorce and a particularly messy breakup as well, Bud's had been the perfect place to escape my lonely, hum-drum lifestyle and make some new friends.

Every Thursday, Friday, and Saturday nights, I could most likely be found sitting at the bar and sipping a cold draft beer and chowing down on some great fried chicken and listening to the jukebox and laughing and cracking jokes and in general just having the time of my life.

It wasn't just the great food and cold beer and all the laughs, either. I used to think that if you had seen one tavern you'd seen them all, but with Bud's, it felt different somehow.

That is, until *that* day.

TWO

When I walked into the tavern that morning, the overall atmosphere was much different than usual.

As soon as I walked in, missing was the usual cheerful banter and laughter, and had been replaced with a air of nervousness and forboding. And, in the middle of it all, sat Mr Dallas Gentry.

Dallas Gentry was born in Pearl City, Indiana, a small, run down community of ramshackle houses and derelict trailers nestled in between the town levee and the Wabash River basin. His mother, Lula, a known alcoholic and brawler, had once sold Dallas in exchange for a carton of cigarettes and a half gallon of whiskey. The woman who'd purchased Dallas had brought him back within two days claiming he wasn't even smart enough to pull a plow or bait a fish hook, and demanded her payment back.

His childhood had been less than pleasant or normal in any way at all.

And it was showing today.

When I walked in, the *only* voice I heard was that of Mr Wallace, loud and boisterous and obviously *drunk*.

As he sat at the bar, gulping down draft beers and regaling the other patrons with tales of his latest escapades – cashing in almost forty-five dollars worth of aluminum cans earlier in the day – everyone else in the place seemed almost entranced by his tale, when, in reality, they were more in fear of him than interested in anything he had to say.

I had to admit, he was a tough looking old fart; big bug eyes, a scarred face, and a deep, raspy voice that sent shivers down your spine whenever he would raise his voice another octave or two.

But his eyes were the most noticeable part of his features.

They seemed to bug out of his head like two hard boiled eggs, bloodshot and empty. When he looked at you, you couldn't tell if he was looking straight at you or past you, or over the top of your head.

It was very creepy to say the least.

#

Anyway, back to the story.

As I walked in, everyone at the bar turned to look at me, flashed me a weak smile, and went back to listening to Dallas brag about his big cash windfall.

I sat at the bar, ordered a beer, and sat listening to him as well, and it hadn't taken me long to get tired of it.

I don't mind listening to someone telling the tall tale – it comes with the territory in a tavern – but, after so long, the *same* story gets tiresome, and I had come in there to *relax*.

After listening to his tale – for the third time in a row – I couldn't take it anymore.

It wasn't because I was jealous of his new found fortune, mind you. I just didn't see any point in repeating the same story over and over again.

I drained my beer, stood up, and calmly walked

around the bar to face him, and said, "Excuse me, sir, but don't you have any *other* stories you can tell? I'm sure you have other tales of drunkenness and ignorance you can entertain us with."

He wheeled around in his barstool, looked me directly in the eyes, and said, "What did you say, you little shit?"

Doing my best to ignore his creepy gaze, I said, "I said, your story is becoming *very* boring, and I came in here to *relax*, not listen to your drunken ramblings all day."

At that very moment, you could have heard a pin drop. The other patrons seemed to gasp for breath, at my bravery – or stupidity, in their eyes.

Dallas said, "If you don't like what I'm talking about, why don't you just get the hell out of here, before I have to stomp your ass?"

Giving him the once over, sizing him up, I could see he had a large hunting knife in a sheath on his ancient leather belt, and I couldn't help but wonder just how many men he'd sliced up with it in the past.

I wasn't going to take any chances.

I forced a smile, extended my hand, and said, "I was just joking, my friend. Please, carry on with your story. I find it quite interesting."

He studied my face for a few moments, he forced a smile and said, "No harm done, I guess."

He didn't shake my hand.

I motioned to the bartender and said, "Give my new friend another beer on me. Hell, make it *two* beers."

At the notion of two free beers, Gentry's whole demeanor changed. He smiled, and said, "Well, thank you friend. That's mighty nice of you."

With that, I'd saved my ass from possibly getting skinned alive, and heard some very tall tales, too.

#

For the next several hours, I sat and listened to Gentry tell me some really tall tales; the time he hopped a train to Memphis, to see Elvis; the time he got in a fight with five Mexicans and whipped their asses; and the time he carried almost forty pounds of aluminum cans over his back for almost two miles to cash them in, among other tales.

I had to admit, for someone who was obviously full of shit, he had a way about him when it came to story telling, managed to be very convincing.

By mid-afternoon, three sheets in the wind and in fear I wouldn't be able to walk home without assistance, I had bid farewell to Gentry and the rest of the gang, and walked back home, with the sun at my back and feeling at least somewhat reinvigorated.

I was asleep on the couch by supper time.

THREE

For the first time in weeks, I slept like a baby.

I woke up around dawn the next day, and, after my usual shit shower and shave routine, I had sat down at my computer again, to see what I could come up with for my great American novel.

As is sat sipping single malt and staring at the screen again, it suddenly hit me that after all of these years, I had yet to finish my novel, or come up with an interesting subject to base it on.

But, never one to be easily defeated, I started typing away, basing my new story on my conversation with Dallas Gentry. If anyone could be considered an interesting subject to write about, it was him.

A few hours later, almost three sheets in the wind, and needing a break, I had adjourned to the front porch to take in some afternoon sunshine and relax my weary mind.

I hadn't been sititng there for long when the paperboy delivered the Wabash Valley Gazette. Upon glancing at the front page headlines, I couldn't believe what I was reading.

Dallas Gentry had been found by one of his neighbors, dead in his home, from a gunshot wound to the back of his head.

So much for relaxing my weary mind.

#

After composing myself, I'd gone back inside, sat down at the kitchen table, lit a cigarette, poured some more single malt, and continued reading the article on Gentry's untimely death.

To my horror, I read that he had shot and robbed for a grand total of less then forty-five dollars, some loose change, and some old yard sale grade jewelry.

I guess life really is cheap.

After reading the article, it had left no doubt as to what my next story would entail; a full length story about my day chatting with Gentry.

But, before I even had a chance to begin, there was a loud knocking at my door.

It was the police – wanting to talk to me about Dallas Gentry.

What a story this was going to be after all.

FOUR

The plain clothes cop who knocked on my door was named Harley Crow.

He was a tall, lanky fella with a big nose and beady little eyes. As we stood in my doorway exchanging social graces, I couldn't help but wonder why all Detectives, whether it be on TV or in real life, were always tall and lanky and had a big nose, but I kept that thought to myself.

As he stepped inside my apartment, I said, "Just take a seat at the table. Want some coffee? It's the instant stuff, but it's okay."

Sitting down, he smiled and said, "No thanks, I won't be here long."

I sat down too, sipped my single malt, and said, "So, Mr Crow. What can I help you with?"

Crow crossed his legs and said, "Mr Polanski, I understand that you spent a few hours yesterday afternoon, chatting with a fellow named Dallas Gentry."

I said, "Yes, I did. Very colorful character, he was, too."

Crow grinned and said, "Yes, he was. Very much so. What was it you fellas talked about all that time, if I may ask?"

I said, "Honestly? He did most of the talking. He had some really tall tales, too. I mostly just sat there and drank beer and listened to him."

Crow said, "Uh huh. So, he didn't do anything but feed you a lot of BS, and that's it? He didn't talk about money or anything else?"

I said, "Well, to be honest, he was flashing his money around, real proud he'd just cashed in some beer cans. I didn't think it was a very good idea, either, considering the crowd."

Crow said, "I have to agree with that," and was looking at me when he said it, like a scientist would study a lab rat. I didn't know whether to take it as an insult or not, so I just said, "Meaning?"

He said, "Meaning *nothing*, Mr Polanski. No offense intended."

I said, "No offense taken. But, I'm going to be very busy today. Is there anything else you want to speak to me about?"

Standing to his feet, Crow lit a cigarette and said, "No, that's all for now. I'm speaking with *all* of the patrons who were there yesterday. It's just a matter of police procedure, Mr Polanski."

Breathing a momentary sigh of relief, I said, "No problem, I understand."

Crow said, "Well, I better get going, I have other people to talk to today."

I walked him to the door, and as he walked out into the hallway, he said, "Mr Polanksi, don't stray too far away. I might need to speak with you again."

I said, "Where would I go?"

Then I shut the door in his face.

And sipped my single malt.

FIVE

By the time I had sipped about a pint's worth of my single malt, it was time for supper.

Having trouble deciding on either stale lunchmeat or TV dinners, I'd opted for a cold beer instead.

Then another.

I had to have some inspiration, you know, if I was to write about Mr Dallas Gentry.

And what better source of inspiration than the hair of the dog that bit me?

I was betting that Dallas would have felt the same about the situation.

So, I drink and I write.

#

By around ten pm, I had come up with about ten pages of the story – Gentry's story – and was pretty satisfied with it, so I decided to call it a night.

I walked out on the front porch, sat down in my ancient lawn chair, and sat gazing up at the full moon.

Except that night, it didn't look like a full moon. It looked like a big white skull, grinning at me, like it knew something I didn't know, something I *should* know, but was going to let the secret stay that way until I found it out for myself, the hard way.

Like always.

So, I sat and drank and stared at the moon and finally fell asleep in my lawn chair, and didn't wake up until almost dawn – and actually woke up hungry.

#

After a breakfast of instant oatmeal I'd found in the cupboard, I'd popped a cold beer and sat back down at my computer for another day of what I was hoping would be some productive writing.

As it turned out, my recent case of writer's block had all but disppeared, and I had a great day.

That is, until I read the newspaper again that afternoon.

Right on the front page was another article on the murder case, and it said that the police had several suspects, but hadn't made any arrests just yet.

The bad thing was, *my* name, well as several other bar partrons, was mentioned in the article as possible "witnesses" at the bar that day, seen chatting with Gentry.

It was then I knew what I had to do; I had to clear my own name – and find out *who* killed Dallas Gentry.

Talk about a great American novel.

SIX

More like the great American shit-show, if I allowed myself to get carried away.

I had to move slow, incognito, so to speak, and keep my head down on this one, didn't want to draw any unwanted attention from Mr Big Nose, Harley Crow.

Since I been listed as one of the "witnesses," the last thing I wanted to do was make him suspicious in any way.

But, first things first.

I had to move very slowly, be slow and meticulous, *methodical*, in the way I was going to approach this situation.

I had to have a *plan*.

#

My plan was this; to wait a few days until things calmed down at the crime scene, then sneak in there after dark, and snoop around for any clues.

I had always been a big fan of magazines like *True Detective*, and TV shows like *Cops* and *Forensic Files*, so I didn't think I'd have any problem playing detective, becoming an "amateur sleuth," so to speak.

I knew by watching *Forensic Files*, that sometimes, the police would miss an unobvious clue, and maybe, just *maybe*, I would be the one to find it.

Now, turning the clue over to the police while remaining anonymous could prove to be difficult, but I'd worry about that later.

Now, on with my plan.

But first, a drink to celebrate!

SEVEN

I had devised my plan on a Tuesday, and had waited until Saturday night to put it into motion.

That night, around midnight, I had my little travel bag ready; a pack of cigarettes, a small flashlight, a black bandana to cover my face, and, of course, a half of single malt for the road.

Just to settle my nerves, you know.

I was ready.

#

As I approached the entrance to Pearl City, I noticed immediately that there were several porch lights on, and a bonfire near one of the trailers that wasn't quite extinguished yet, so I knew I couldn't just walk right in like I owned the place without being seen.

So, I had decided to come in from the back side, scaling the river levee and coming in from behind, shrouded in darkness and concealed by trees and tall weeds.

It worked.

As I descended the levee from the back, right behind Gentry's old cabin, I could see yellow crime scene tape was still surrounding the place, draped between several trees.

I walked down the levee, watching where I

stepped so I wouldn't fall down and bust my ass. By the time I reached the back of the cabin, I felt as though I was home free.

For the time being, that is.

I stopped, took a sip from the half pint, lit a cigarette, took a deep breath, and ducked under the yellow tape.

Once inside, having gained access by crawling through a back window, I turned my small flashlight on, and began training the dim yellow beam on my current location, which was apparently the bedroom.

It was a tiny little room, not more than ten by twelve feet in diameter, and the only furniture was a small, lumpy, sweat stained mattress on the floor, and a small nightstand, fashioned from an old wooden crate, sitting nearby.

Mr Dallas Gentry had lived a very meager existence at best.

Then I saw the blood stains.

On the top of the mattress, dried now, appearing almost black in the moonlight shining through the window.

The very spot where Mr Dallas Gentry, a poor old man with not many friends or a pet or very much money, had met his untimely end by being shot in the head as he slept, by a coward who knew they couldn't handle him if he was awake – and brandishing his knife.

I tried blocking the image from my mind as best I could, and moved on to the next room.

The bathroom.

Or, what could pass for a bathroom, that is.

It was smaller than the bedroom in size, very cramped and uncomfortable.

The only furnishings was a small, dirty bathtub, a sink, and an ancient toilet that looked as though it had been manufactured at least fifty years ago.

He must not have had any running water, except for a ground pump outside, because sitting next to the toilet was an old five gallon bucket he must have used to flush the toilet, and haul water in to take a bath.

In the next room, was his so called "living room" area, complete with an old tattred couch, a small coffee table with an overflowing ashtray resting on top, a few empty beer cans, and an old newspaper.

Close by, resting atop an old folding table, was a Coleman stove, I guess he used to heat up or cook his meager diet.

That was it.

Dallas Gentry's whole life in a nutshell.

Which hadn't been much, but it had meant the whole world to him.

Just like my own meager lifestyle meant to much to me, too.

It was at that very moment, that all thoughts of how much he'd gotten on my nerves that day, and his loud, raspy voice and big bug eyes didn't mean shit to me anymore.

I felt *guilty*.

As I very well should have.

But now, I was going to try and make things right again, if that was possible, or at least die trying.

I'd almost lost my life to cancer – twice, as a matter of fact – so I wasn't going to allow Mr Harley Big Nose Crow to stop me from conducting my own little investigation.

I had already come too far to back out now.

So, gathering my thoughts as well as my cigarette butts – didn't want to leave any evidence of my nocturnal visit behind – I started to leave the way I came in, when a thought suddenly came to mind that stopped me dead in my tracks.

Cigarette butts.

I hadn't seen Gentry smoking the day of our little chat.

Yet, his living room was *full* of cigarette butts.

Could at least *some* of those butts be from his killer?

Could this asshole have been so cold and heartless that he just sat down, kicked back, and drank a few of Gentry's beers and smoked a few cigarettes before he left?

Like there was nothing at all out of the ordinary by doing so?

What a piece of shit, I thought, angrily. *What a piece of human waste.*

Who *are* you?

I damn well intended to find out.

EIGHT

I made it home around three am.

The first thing I did was pop a cold beer, sit down at the computer, and type up a new "case file" about what I'd seen at the cabin.

Then I took a shot of single malt, hit the couch, and didn't wake up until the next day – when I heard a loud knocking at my door.

#

It was Mr Harley Crow.

By the time I'd dragged my lazy half drunk ass off of the couch and opened the door, he had begun knocking loud enough to wake the dead.

Upon yanking the door open, ready to let loose with a whole slew of colorful comments, he had beat me to it, saying, "Wow, I must say, Mr Polanski, you've looked better."

Holding my tongue, I said, "That's real funny. Are you moonlighting as a stand up comic now?"

Crow grinned and said, "No, but I heard you've been moonlighting down at Pearl City."

Feigning ignorance, of course, I said, "What in the hell are you talking about?"

He said, "May I come in? Or would you rather me embarrass you in front of your neighbors?"

I motioned to him to come in, as I walked into the kitchen and sat down at the table, pouring myself a shot of single malt. As I sipped the liquid salvation, he sat down, lit a cigarette, and said, "What? No corn flakes with your whiskey?"

Taking another sip, I said, "I had a hard night last night, if that's any of your business."

Crow said, "It may very well be my business, if you were snooping around Gentry's old cabin last night."

I said, "I was home all night last night. I watched some TV, had something to eat, and didn't wake up until you were beating on my door."

Crow said, "Hmm...well, that's funny, because one of Gentry's old neighbors said they saw someone snooping around the cabin right after midnight, and the description they gave me matches you almost exactly."

Shaking my head, I said, "Well, I must have a doppleganger then, because it wasn't me."

Crow cracked a cocky grin and said, "Oh my, an exact twin to Mr Charles Polanski. That's a frightening thought."

I grinned and said, "Yes it is, isn't it?"

Crow's grin furrowed into a frown as he said, "Look, Mr Polanski. I can't prove it was you snooping around down there, but I will say this; if I catch you snooping around down there, I will *arrest* you, and charge you with trespassing, and obstruction."

I said, "Point taken. Anything else? I have a terrible hangover."

Standing to his feet, Crow said, "That's it, for *now*, that is. Just remember what I said."

With that, Crow walked to the door, opened it,

and turned to look back at me as I walked up behind him. He said, "Remember, Mr Polanksi, stay *away* from my crime scene."

As he walked down the hallway, I said, "Mr Crow?"

He stopped and said, "Yeah?"

I said, "Why don't you go screw yourself?"

Then I slammed the door, locked it, and went back to work on my case file.

NINE

I had stopped long enough to take a shower, and then I was right back to work on the case file.

There wasn't much to it just yet; just a general outline, of what I saw at the cabin, and the discarded cigarette butts I saw on the coffee table.

Looking back on that night again, it had come to me that the beer cans I'd seen strewn about were Bucdweiser, and I knew that Gentry preferred the cheaper brands, like Strohs and Pabst Blue Ribbon.

So why were there *Budweiser* beer cans there? I mean, sure, he could have a friend drop by, who preferred Budweiser. But for some reason, I didn't believe in that theory.

So...on with the case file!

#

By around noon, I had taken a break, popped a cold beer, and walked outside to enjoy the sunshine for a little while.

As I sat down in my ancient lawn chair, lit a cigarette and sipped my beer, my peace and solitude was suddenly interrupted by the sound of a loud voice coming from nearby.

I turned to see my next door neighbor, Rick Pickle, yelling and cursing at the top of his lungs – and, waving a *gun* in the air.

Knowing that the gun was a 41 magnum, I knew what a huge hole it could leave behind when it pierced human flesh.

Also being aware of what a "pickle" Rick could be when he had too much to drink, I thought I'd better intervene before he accidently shot someone.

As I walked off of the porch steps, he suddenly wheeled around, pointed the gun right at my face, and said, "Watch it, Chuck! I'm not fucking around!"

I stopped, cleared my throat, and said, "No problem, neighbor. So...what seems to be the problem today?"

Lowering the gun a bit, he said, "What else?! My old lady!"

Ah...I thought. *His old lady.*

His wife, Rita.

He'd found out last year that she'd been unfaithful to him, and he'd totally flipped out. I can't say I blame him, but, she wasn't worth going to prison.

The author Charles Bukowski once said, "Find what you love, and let it kill you." But, I doubt he was referring to one's love life.

And yet women — good women — frightened me because they eventually wanted your soul, and what was left of mine, I wanted to keep. So...I couldn't honestly give him any good advice on how to handle his current problem with Rita, but I could try to calm him down – and try to disarm him.

I said, "Rick, I don't have any idea what Rita has done to you this time, but it isn't worth going to jail."

He took a deep breath and said, "It ain't worth jail, or my life."

The he raised the gun and pointed it at his head.

He cocked the hammer back, and closed his tear filled eyes.

That's when I lunged forward, using my left arm to push the gun away, and use my right arm – my hand – to push him backward.

The gun went off, the bullet striking a nearby tree.

He landed hard, on his ass, knocking the wind out of him.

I reached out and snatched the gun out of his hand, and tossed it out of reach. As he lay squirming to get free, some of the other neighbors were gathering around by then, one of them dialing 911 no doubt. As two of my other neighbors detained him as they waited for the police to arrive, I made my exit – and fast.

I had no doubt Mr Harley Crow would show up, and, seeing me in the middle of it all, would surely want to give me a hard time.

So...I got up, kicking the gun even further away, and walked inside the building without saying a word. I ducked inside, locked the door behind me, and sat at the kitchen table, sipping single malt and hoping – praying – that Crow wouldn't show up.

No such luck.

TEN

It wasn't more than a few minutes later when the loud rapping at my door began.

I could always recognize his knock more than anyone else's; so loud, so...purposeful.

So...angry.

It was like there was code behind his knock, and once it was deciphered, it would say *Open this door Mr Polanski before I kick it in!*

So, I took a deep breath, exhaled, lit a cigarette, and yanked the door open. There stood Crow, his face bathed in sweat, and looking at me like I was nothing more than a bug – a bug he'd like to stomp on.

He said, "Well, Mr Polanski. I see you have managed to get yourself into trouble again."

I said, "I don't *even* know what in the hell you're talking about."

Crow's beady little eyes focused in on my own, like he could see right through me, and he said, "Don't play dumb with me. I know you were outside just a few minutes ago, in the thick of it all."

I said, "If you are referring to the incident with Mr Pickle, I merely disarmed him before he could kill someone – or himself."

Crow lit a cigarette and said, "My point is, you seem to *always* be in the middle of something these days. Can't stay out of trouble."

I said, "Trouble has followed me all of my life, Mr Crow. No reason it should be any different now."

Crow looked at me for a few seconds, like he was a scientist examining a lab rat. He said, "Just exactly *who* are you, Mr Polanski? Or better yet, *what* are you?"

I said, "Honestly?"

He shook his head and said, "I wouldn't have asked otherwise."

I stepped forward, staring him down, and said, "I am the grand master of disaster. I am the baddest Billy-Bad-Ass on the block. I am the HMIC – head motherfucker in charge."

Crow stepped back and said, "Come again?"

I sipped my single malt and said, "I'm usually a very easy going guy, believe it or not. But if you mess with me – or anyone I love, God forbid – I can be the nightmare you *never* want to have."

Crow was speechless at first, then he said, "Why are you telling me this? It doesn't exactly improve my outlook toward you."

I said, "I'm just being *honest*, that's all. I can be the nightmare that walks and talks and will always be there when you wake up. But instead, I choose to stay to myself, don't bother anyone else, and mind my own business. In other words, Mr Crow, you are harrassing me for no reason."

Crow said, "I'm not harrassing you, Mr Polanksi, I'm just doing my job."

I said, "Well, you've done your job, and I am going to bid you farewell for now. Like I told you before, I'm very busy lately."

Stomping his cigarette out on the hallway floor, Crow said, "Ah, yes. The aspiring writer. So, what is your new book about, if I may ask?"

I said, "You may ask, but I don't think it's any of your business, Mr Crow. Is there anything else before I slam this door in your face?"

He said, sarcastically, "Yes. Why don't you go screw yourself?"

I slammed the door.

ELEVEN

It's always been this way, as long as I can remember.

I can haunt you in the midnight and come after you with an upraised scythe like the Grim Reaper. I can reach out and touch you no matter where you hide, whether you are a pedophile priest or a drug dealer or a wife beater or even the President of the United States.

I can find out what books you read what porn movies you rent, your favorite brand of liquor, or the dosing schedule for your Prozac prescription.

I'm the Devil, and I'm God. I am the guy who can sign your hall passes from Purgatory. I smile a dark smile when you nervously try to convince yourself that I won't find you.

But most of all, I'm just Chuck Polanski, orphan and alcoholic and aspiring writer, just looking for a way to get through each day without wanting to eat a bullet.

So, I move on.

#

First, a cold beer, then a shower, then back to work on my case file.

Not much yet, but it's getting there.

So far, I most definitely have enough info – even if it is what you could consider "circumstantial" evidence – to form my own theory as to what happened that night at Gentry's cabin.

My own theory is, Dallas had spent too much time that day at the bar, flashing his money around, and had attracted the unwanted attention of another patron – or patrons – and he or they had come up with a plan to rob him later that night – but, somewhere along the way, the killer or killers had decide that it would be better just to shoot him and get it over with, so he couldn't defend himself.

Even a low life dirtbag was smart enough to know that old Dallas could have ripped them a new ass with that big hunting knife, and were too cowardly to face him down, anyway.

Hence, the well placed bullet in the back of his head.

Infamous Western outlaw, John Wesley Hardin once said, "A bullet to the front of the head demonstrates good marksmanship. A bullet to the back of the head demonstrates good judgement."

In my opinion, his killer or killers had demonstrated the same cowardly judgement that night, opting to shoot him from behind – and while he was alseep, no less.

The motive behind it all was obvious.

Now, I just had to figure out *who* it was that had been such a cowardly piece of shit.

So, I had decided to begin my investigation by paying a visit to the local tavern, where I was sure it had all began.

TWELVE

It was a sunny day that day, with a slight breeze and temperatures in the mid seventies.

A perfect day for a walk – and an investigation.

As I sauntered into the bar with notepad and pen in hand, I saw that I was the first patron of the day, just me and the bartender, Cindra. That was fine with me; I didn't need an audience to be eavesdropping on our conversation.

As I sat down at the bar, Cindra said, "Well, if it isn't the neighborhood writer. Working on anything interesting?"

I said, "Maybe, maybe not. That really might depend on what you may tell me."

Seeming confused, she said, "Come again?"

I lit a cigarette and said, "The last time I was here, you know, the day me and Dallas sat there drinking beer and chatting?"

She said, "Yeah, what about it?"

I leaned in and said, "Well, can you remember who all was here that day? I man, was there anyone here that *wasn't* a regular customer?"

Seeming more suspicious than confused now, she said, "Why do you ask?"

I said, "Just curious is all."

She said, "Hell, Chuck, that was days ago, you know? I can't remember everyone that was here that day."

I said, "Are you sure? I mean, it would really help me out."

Glancing at my notepad and pen, she said, "Oh, don't tell me. You are writing a story about what happened to Dallas gentry, aren't you?"

Feigning ignorance, I said, "What makes you say that?"

She said, "I heard about it. Some tall, big nosed cop with a surly attitude has been here several times, asking the same questions and even mentioned your name more than once."

Great, I thought, glumly. *Crow is bound and determined to screw this up for me. He was smarter than I'd given him credit for.*

I lied and said, "I'm just writing a story on it, to sell to the local newspaper, that's all."

She said, "Chuck, I don't mind serving you beer and going through the obligatory social graces, but otherwise, I watch thy own ass. I have bills to pay and kids to feed."

Giving into defeat, I said, "That's okay. I understand, really I do."

Wiping the bar down, she said, "Is there anything else? We have draft beers today, for fifty cents."

I forced a smile and said, "Thanks, but I better get going."

As I stood to leave, she said, "Chuck?"

I said, "Yeah?"

She said, "Good luck with your story. I really mean that, too."

I said, "Thank you, Cindra. I wish you the best too."

Then I walked out the door, back toward home, feeling defeated once again, and ready to get drunk.
So that's exactly what I did.

THIRTEEN

Feeling defeated – momentarily – I had lost my grip on reality once again, and took refuge inside of a bottle.

I had one of my blackout spells, too.

I woke up that night around ten pm, somewhat the worse for wear, but still alive.

I had begun to think that the fact I was still alive was done by divine intervention; the Lord, in all of his infinite wisdom, had placed a curse on me. The curse of staying alive, almost immortal to the demon alcohol, doomed to suffer the consequences of my actions until the very day I took the long dirt nap.

I guess I'd find out someday.

But, for now, it was back to work.

But, first things first; go into the bathroom, puke my guts out, take a long hot shower, pop a cold beer, and come up with a whole new strategy.

#

While I was in the shower, the next move in my quest had hit me like a ton of bricks.

Why not go to the *main source* for some possible answers?

Talk to the neighbor that had found Gentry's body.

But the big question would be, which neighbor was it?

I hoped to find that out soon enough – and without Mr Harley Crow's interference.

#

After I'd gotten my hangover under control, I'd packed a half pint in my boot and headed toward Pearl City.

It was another sunny day, with a nice breeze and fluffy white clouds, and a chance of rain in the afternoon.

Rain, gloomy days, never bothered me much; I just figured it was God's way of washing all of the scum – human and otherwise – down the sewer drains, making room for some more beauty in the world.

I hoped I was right.

As I entered the main dirt road into Pearl City, I had immediately noticed the lack of it's residents milling about.

Normally, the residents of Pearl City were up with the first light, watering their plants or mowing their lawn or sitting on the porch chatting, some of them down at the river's edge fishing for their dinner.

But that day, the place seemed deserted. I didn't even hear a dog barking or a fly buzzing in the air.

It was like Gentry's death, so close to home, had frightened the other residents into laying low and keeping their heads down – but hiding from what?

Or who?

I guess I'd find out soon enough.

As I walked along, glancing from left to right for any signs of life, I looked up to see an attractive, blonde haired lady of around forty years old, sitting on the front steps of decent looking house trailer, smoking a cigarette and sipping coffee.

Before I even had a chance to wave or say good morning, she took a sip of her coffee, and said, "Are you looking for anything or anyone in particular?"

Taken back by the remark at first, I cleared my throat and said, "As a matter of fact, I am."

She said, "A person or a thing?"

I said, "A person."

She said, "Anyone in particular? I've lived here most of my life, most likely know them."

Not being in the mood to beat around the bush, I said, "I'm looking for the person who found Dallas Gentry's body."

Expecting a deer in the headlights look, one of surprise, catching her off guard, all I received was a simple shrug of the shoulders and the remark, "Well, good luck, then."

She stood up, poured what was left of her coffee in the dirt, and started to walk back inside the trailer. I stepped closer and said, "Excuse me, ma'am?"

She turned back to me, hesitantly, and said, "You are the guy, aren't you?"

"The guy?" I said, confused.

She lit another cigarette and said, "The guy who has been snooping around here after dark. The aspiring writer."

She had me dead to rights on that one. I said, "Yes, ma'am, that would be me."

She seemed to relax a bit, and said, "Don't keep calling me ma'am. I'm not an old lady, you know."

I smiled at her remark and said, "Excuse me, Miss?"

She said, "Patricia Lang. My friends just call me

Patty."

I said, "And what should I call you?"

She cracked a smile too, and said, "Well, Mr aspiring writer, if you intend to interrogate me, why not just call me Patty?"

I said, "Patty it is. And I'm Chuck Polanski, pleased to make your acquaintance."

Still grinning, she said, "You may not be so pleased soon enough. Come on in, I need a refill on my coffee."

So into the trailer I went, but keeping my guard up just in case.

FOURTEEN

The inside of her trailer was immaculate.

Everything was clean and shiny and in it's proper place. I pictured her as divorced, single, and spent most of her time smoking, drinking coffee and cleaning house to chase the blues away.

I knew how she felt all too well.

As she poured some more coffee, she said, "Just take a seat at he kitchen table if you want. Coffee? It's fresh."

Sitting down at the table, I said, ""No thank you. It tends to upset my stomach this early in the day."

She sat down grinning, and said, "Yeah, a bad hangover will do that."

Feeling slightly embarrassed, I said, "How could you tell?"

She said, "My ex was a drunk. Not that he was bad person, you know? He just had a monkey on his back."

I said, "I know the feeling."

She said, "So, Mr Polanski, you were asking about the person who found Dal's body?"

Lighting a cigarette, I said, "Yes, if you don't mind."

She leaned back in her chair, sipped her coffee, cleared her throat, and said, "That would be me."

I said, "Come again?"

She said, "It was me that found him. My son, Milton, and I were pretty close with Dallas, and kept an eye on him from time to time, to make sure he was okay."

I said, "So, how did it happen, exactly?"

She said, "Well, my son came home that day, and told me that Dallas was walking around here, bragging about his big score on aluminum cans. That day was his social security day, too, so he had a lot more money in his pocket than anyone knew about. Or, at least *one* perosn knew, anyway."

I said, "Your son, Milton? Did he warn Dallas to stop bragging, and sober up?"

She said, "Oh yeah. But as usual, when Dallas was on a binge, and feeling his oats, nobody could tell him shit. A stubborn old bastard, he was."

I said, "So, you went to check on him that night, and found him dead?"

Fighting back tears, she said, "Yes. It was around ten o'clock. When he didn't answer the door, I feared the worst, and walked inside, knowing that he wouldn't mind me stopping by. I found him in the bedroom, with a gunshot in the back of his head."

I said, "I'm so sorry you had to see that."

Blinking away tears, she said, "Me too."

She said, "You know what else is so sad about this? Since then, most folks that live here, they avoid my son and I like the plague. Like we had something to do with it."

I said, "Small town rumor and gossip, it never fails."

She said, "Tell me about it."

I said, "I could use a drink. How about you?"

She said, "Sorry, I haven't been to the store lately, or I'd offer you one."

I reached down, retrieved the half pint from my boot, and said, "I have us covered."

Cracking a smile then, she scooted her coffee cup across the table, and said, "Please, fill me up."

So I did – and filled my cup as well.

FIFTEEN

Our next chat was very interesting to say the least.

Over the next several hours, she had filled me in on her whole life history, from her less than happy childhood until her adult years, when she'd married Milton's father, and their subsequent divorce because of his alcoholism.

By the time she was finished, I felt as though I'd known her forever – had found a kindred spirit, so to speak – someone I had a lot in common with.

By then, the half pint was empty, too.

Noticing this, she suggested that we walk down to the package store for a refill – and she would pay for it.

A woman after my own heart.

Yet another lost soul, searching for something or aomeone they never really find, but keep on looking anyway, and have some fun along the way.

Like today.

Or so I'd thought at the time.

#

We had decided to go to my place on the way back – not only because it was closer, but also because we were in fear of being arrested for public intoxication otherwise.

As we sat at my tiny table, sharing more drinks and cheerful banter, she'd noticed my old laptop and and said, "So, I guess that's where all of the magic happens, huh?"

I said, "I don't know about magic, but I do my best."

She sipped her drink and said, "So, are you going to let me in on the case file you were telling me about, or not?"

Reluctantly, I said, "Well, okay, but you have to promise not to tell *anyone* about it."

She crossed her fingers, and said, jokingly, "Cross my heart and hope to die."

I said, "Okay, follow me."

As I sat down and booted up the laptop, with her standing over my shoulder, she said, "So, are you *really* a private investigator, or just playing one?"

I said, "More like the latter," and opened the case file. After glancing at it for just a few seconds, she backed away a bit, and said, "You know, I better get home. My son will be coming home soon, and I promised him a catfish dinner today."

As I stood up and faced her, her face was flushed, and her eyes were darting around nervously. You would think she had seen a ghost.

I said, "Is something wrong? I'm sorry if I have offended you in some way."

Lying to my face, she said, "Oh no, it's not that. I just promised my son, that's all."

Then she turned away, walking toward the door, without another word. Gone was the big smile and friendly personality and she couldn't wait to get out of there.

Before I could even say goodbye, she slammed the door behind her, and was gone. I walked to the front window and peeked out, to see her running now, running like the wind, as if to escape something that had terrified her.

I sat back down at the laptop, to see where I had stopped scrolling, and it was the paragraph about finding the beer cans and cigarette butts.

Why would that spook her so bad? I thought, dumbfounded.

I very well intended to find out the next day.

But before I had a chance, Mr Crow came by to see me.

SIXTEEN

That next morning, as I sat at the kitchen table indulging in some Corn Flakes and beer { I had run out of milk, so sue me} I suddenly heard that loud, repetitious knocking again, and did my best to ignore it.

But the longer I sat there shoveling Corn Flakes into my mouth, the louder and harder he knocked, until I thought the door would come loose from it's hinges.

I stood up, kicking my chair across the room, and stomped to the door, yanking it open and saying, "Yes, Mr Crow?! What can I do for you today?!"

Sensing my frustration, he cracked a big shit eating grin and said, "Good morning, Mr Polanski. I hope I didn't interrupt anything important."

I took a deep breath, exhaled, and said, "As a matter of fact, I was in the middle of eating breakfast."

He said, "You actually eating breakfast? I thought you'd be on your liquid diet by this time of the morning."

Doing my best to hold my temper, I said, "Real funny, Crow. I still say you would be a great standup comic."

He grinned and said, "I've heard that before, but I'm too busy chasing your silly ass all over the place to pursue my dreams of becoming rich and famous."

I said, "You're breaking my heart, Crow. Is there anything special you want to talk about, before I finish my soggy Corn Flakes?"

He said, "As a matter of fact, I do. I heard a vicious rumor that you were snooping around Pearl City yesterday morning. I thought to myself, no, that can't be true, because I told him to *stop* snooping around down there."

Lying through my teeth, of course, I said, "Listen, Crow, I got bored sitting around here, so I took a long walk. I had heard the fishing was good down there, too, so I dropped by there to check it out."

Crow said, "Was part of your fishing expedition dropping by Patty Lang's place?"

I said, "I was strolling by her place, and she spoke to me. That's all. It was just being sociable."

Crow said, "You both must have been feeling *real* sociable, to leave together and hit the neighborhood liquor store."

I said, "Crow, what I do and who I do it with is none of your damned business."

He said, "It is when it is obstructing my current investigation."

I said, "And just how in the hell am I obstructing anything?"

He said, "Just by being in the thick of it all is enough to arrest you. Now, am I going to have to lock your goofy ass up in jail for a while, or are you going to stop snooping around Pearl City? This investigation could take months, or even years. For some reason, I don't think you'd last that long in county lockup without losing your composure."

He was right about that. I'd done time in jail before, and I hated every second of it.

I lied again and said, "Fine. No more visits to

Pearl City. Anything else?"

He said, "Yes, there is. Stay away from Patty Lang too, and her worthless son. Believe me, Polanksi, they would be nothing but trouble for you."

Lying yet again, I said, "Fine, no more chasing coochie down at Pearl City. Can I finish my breakfast now?"

Studying my face again, he said, "Okay, Polanski, but this is your *last* warning. If I catch you down there again, you'll be wearing a striped orange jumpsuit and eating day old dougnuts for breakfast instead of Corn Flakes."

I said, "Are you finished?"

He said, "For *now*, yes."

I slammed the door in his face, and went back to my soggy cereal. Having lost the taste for it, I popped a beer instead, and sat down at my laptop for a while.

About an hour later, I was thumbing through the local phone book for Patty's number.

SEVENTEEN

I knew most folks had cell phones these days, but I knew some of the residents of Pearl City still had land lines, so I took a chance.

To my surprise, there she was:

Patricia Lang
Trailer no. 3
Pearl City Drive.
812 888 4082

I sat back, drained my beer, poured some single malt, and dialed her number.

She answered on the third ring. "Hello?"

Not a friendly tone of voice, more of an inquisitive tone, as though she had no idea of who would want to call her for any reason.

I said, "Patty? It's Chuck."

There was few moments of total silence, and she said, "I'm sorry about yesterday."

I said, "No big deal. I wouldn't want you to break a promise to your son."

She said, "Thank you."

I said, "You know, I was just wondering, how would you like to come by later for a cookout? Nothing facny, just some burgers and homemade fries. My treat."

There was total silence on her end again, then,

"You know, that sounds like fun. What time were you thinking?"

I glanced at my old wristwatch and said, "How about three o'clock?"

She said, "It's a date."

She hung up without saying goodbye, but I didn't think much of it.

#

She showed up around two-thirty, carrying a homemade apple pie with her for dessert.

I took that as a good sign, and felt less nervous than before, but still kept my fingers crossed.

An hour later, as we sat at the small community picnic table eating burgers and sipping cold beer, I couldn't hold back any longer, my curiosity getting the best of me, and asked her, "Tell me, why did you leave the other day like you did?"

She sipped her beer and said, "I thought I already explained that to you."

I said, "I know what you said, but I just had the strong feeling that there was more to it."

She said, nervously, "I said, that was *all* there was to it, okay? Can we just eat our food and have a good day?"

"Sure," I said, taking a bite of my burger. "Sorry about that."

"No harm done," she said, draining her beer. She had seemed to have lost any interest in eating.

There was an uncomfortable silence between us for the next several minutes, until suddenly, right out of the blue, she broke down sobbing and shaking.

The tears seemed to flow like a river, her upper body shaking as though she was having a seizure. I stood up and said, "I'm sorry, Patty. Are you going to be okay?"

After a few moments she managed to gather her composure, and said, "No, *nothing* is okay right now."

I sat back down, sipped my beer, and said, "What is it, Patty? You can tell me."

She leaned in, whispering, and said, "It's about my son, Milton."

I said, "What about him? Did he get into trouble?"

She said, "If I tell you something, do you *promise* to keep it a secret?"

I said, "Sure," but later wished I hadn't.

She said, "The other night, the night that I found Dallas dead? Milton had come home earlier that night, all scared and sweaty and upset. He said his cousin, Ronny Coy, had done something terrible."

I lit a cigarette and said, "Such as?"

She said, You *promise* to keep your mouth shut until I'm sure?"

"Sure of what?" I said, sipping my beer, and wishing it was a glass of single malt. "Just tell me, Patty."

She said, "I think his cousin is the one who shot Dallas Gentry."

Speechless at first, I took another sip of my beer and said, "Was Milton there when he did it?"

Patty wiped her eyes with a napkin and said, "I'm not sure yet, but I think so."

I said, "What exactly did Milton say?"

She began whispering again, saying, "All he said was, Ronny had been at the tavern that day, and some old guy was flashing money around, so he decided to rob him."

I said, "And Milton was with him?"

She said, "He didn't say. But he has been staying away from home a lot, like he's trying to hide out somewhere. My neighbor, Mrs Edwards, told me she saw him and Ronny last night, snooping around the cabin again."

I said, "Maybe Ronny forgot something, like evidence, and went back to get it."

She said, "Like Budweiser beer cans?"

I said, "Yes, exactly. I know Dallas didn't drink that brand."

She said, "But Ronny does – and so does Milton."

I said, "Have you told anybody else besides me?"

She said, "No, not yet."

I said, "Then don't. At least not until I can figure out how to handle this situation."

She said, "What's to handle? You either keep it a secret, or you don't. You *promised*."

I said, "Yes, I did. But Ronny shouldn't be allowed to get away with *murder*, either."

She said, "Yes, but if my son's name is mentioned in your story, he will be considered an "accessory" to the crime too."

I said, "I know that, and I promise, I will keep your son's name *out* of it."

She began sobbing again, walked around the picnic table, and gave me a big hug. She said, "Thank you, Chuck. Thank you so much."

I hugged her back, of course, and while I held her there, I knew at that very moment that I was going to break her heart in the end.

It always ends up the same.

I find someone I have something in common with, someone I think I could actually love, and then they are gone like a puff of smoke.

Sometimes, I think I was *born* to be alone.

EIGHTEEN

It never fails, in the end.

I had thought I had already fallen in love with her, that day I held her by the picnic table. It was like the moment I touched her, an electric charge coarsed through my entire body, awakening long dormant feelings I had thought were lost forever.

I loved like a man loves a woman he never touches, only writes to, keeps little photographs of. Right there, yet for some reason, out of reach.

But Patty's eyes — they're beautiful. They're wild, crazy, like some animal peering out of a forest on fire. Yet, calm and soothing to peer into. Like a huge blue ocean with nothing visible on the horizon but an endless array of day dreams I knew would never come true.

I knew then that I was going to lose her, because I knew I couldn't just let the story end by allowing a murderer to go free – just to satisfy my own lust for a beautiful woman I really didn't know.

So, after she left that day, I got drunk, fell asleep on the couch, and the next day, did something I never would have dreamed of doing otherwise.

I called Harley Crow.

NINETEEN

Needless to say, Crow was very surprised to hear from yours truly.

When you drank the world was still out there, but for the moment it didn't have you by the throat. So I made sure I was good and buzzed before his arrival.

#

When he arrived, I had left the door open and was sitting at the kitchen table, nursing a glass of single malt and smoking a cigarette.

I heard the usual loud rapping at the door, and said, "It's open, Crow." A few seconds later, there he was, standing in my kitchen, big nose and all. He lit a cigarette and said, "So, Mr Polanksi, what was so damned important I couldn't even finish my McMuffin this morning?"

I said, "That fast food will kill you, Crow."

He sat down and said, "This coming from a guy who pours beer on his Corn Flakes."

I said, "Fair enough."

He said, "I'm waiting, Polanski. You said you had something to tell me?"

I said, "How's the Gentry case going? Anything new?"

He narrowed his beady little eyes at me, and said,

"I thought I had told you to back off. Are you just bound and determined to go to jail?"

I smiled and said, "I have some very interesting information, if you want to hear it."

Studying my face for a moment, he said, "Okay, I'm listening."

I said, "I heard it through the Pearl City grapevine, that a young fellow named Ronny Coy is behind Gentry's death."

Crow's facial expression changed from one of boredom to extreme interest then. He said, "Go on."

I said, "If what I heard was true, apparently Coy was at the bar that day, watching Gentry flashing his money around, and had decided to follow him home and rob him."

Crow said, "Sounds like an interesting theory, yes. But, just who was your source?"

I said, "I promised them I would keep their name out of it. Sorry."

Crow said, "Listen, asshole. I have to know who your source is, to see if I think it's worth pursuing. And keep in mind what I said about being charged with obstruction, too."

I said, "Oh, I have. But if I tell you, and it doesn't pan out, then I have broken my promise."

Pulling a pair of handcuffs from the front pocket of his suit jacket, he said, "I'm waiting, asshole."

Not wanting to break my promise, but not wanting to go to jail, either, I reluctantly gave in. I said, "Okay, you win. But, you did not hear it from me. Deal?"

Placing the handcuffs on the table, he said, "Deal. Now, who is it?"

My heart sinking in my chest, I said, "It was Patty Lang."

Crow said, "What did I tell you about that bunch? They're full of shit. They're about as dependable as a broken condom."

I said, "I'm just telling you what I was told. You can pursue it, or not."

Putting his cigarette out in the ashtray, Crow said, "Okay, Mr investigator, I'll look into it. But in the future, whether this pans out or not, keep your ass *away* from this case. You got it?"

Grinning, I said, "I promise."

Standing to his feet, Crow said, "Yeah, and I can see what your promises are worth."

With that, he was gone.

I sat there for a few minutes, just staring at the open door. Then I closed the door, locked it, and got drunker than a barrel full of retarded monkeys.

TWENTY

The next day, I woke up more feeling more ashamed – and guilty – than hungover.

I heard once that in the sun or in the rain, in the day or in the night, pain was a flower, pain is *flowers*, blooming all the time.

If that was true, then my own private pain garden was blooming twenty four hours a day.

That's what I felt that day; pure, deep rooted, unadulterated pain and agony, over breaking my promise to Patty.

But the day wasn't over just yet.

#

Apparently, Crow had left here and gone straight to Patty's trailer, and had proceeded to interrogate her until she finally gave in and admitted her suspicions to him.

Within just a few hours, Milton Lang had been located and arrested for accessory after the fact in a murder case, and Ronny was arrested for first degree murder.

An hour or so later, around dusk, Patty, having taken a handful of pain pills and chased them down with liquor, had proceeded to walk outside, and, standing right in her front yard, pointed a .22 caliber pistol at her head and pulled the trigger, killing her almost instantly.

The next day, as I sat at my computer, just staring at the so called case file, I sick to my stomach at the thought of what horror she went through, the guilt and shame, at telling Crow her son had been involved.

At that moment, I had become violently ill, and had barely made it to the bathroom before voiding my guts.

Then, as usual, I got drunk.

And so it goes.

TWENTY ONE

Milton Lang was convicted and sentenced to thirty years in prison. He would be fifty years old when he was released – that is, if he made it out alive.

Young handsome boys sometimes became targets for the sexual predators in prison, and don't make it out alive – or, at least not in one piece, mentally and physically.

Ronny Coy was convicted of first degree murder, and sentenced to sixty years in prison. He would eighty years old when he was released, which was doubtful. He would most likely die in prison, and be buried in a pauper's grave on the prison grounds, alone and forgotten.

Just like Dallas Gentry had been right before his untimely death. Somehow, Coy's punishment seemed befitting of the crime, in that particular aspect.

But, life goes on.

#

Unfortunately, it goes on for me, too.

That is, what I can possibly salvage of it after this unholy madness.

Each and every time I thought I'd already been through hell and back, I would manage to find myself in yet another crazy situation, that made my previous experiences seem mild in comparison.

Or so I'd thought at the time.

#

Considering my past history, I should have known that this most recent story wasn't over yet.

Sure enough, one day, as I sat on the front porch relaxing in the mid day sunshine, sipping cold beer and listening to the birdies sing, a familiar Sedan pulled up out front.

Out climbed Mr Harley Crow, of course, big nose and all.

Upon seeking him climbing out of the Sedan, I had immediately stood up and headed toward my apartment door, but it was too late. He had already reached the steps and said, "Mr Polanski? I need to talk with you."

I stopped dead in my tracks, turned to face him, and said, "Haven't you talked enough already?"

Lighting a cigarette, Crow said, "Meaning?"

Trying me best to maintain my composure, I said, "Like you talked to *Patty*. Like you talked to her the day she *killed* herself."

Crow lowered his head in shame, and said, "I know, Polanksi. But I had no idea she was that unstable."

I lit a cigarette and said, "Wouldn't *you* be unstable, after all she'd been through? I can just see it now, you sitting there, staring her down, intimdating her into telling you her story. Fucking with her, just like you fucked with me."

He said, "Polanski, I didn't come here to discuss

my obvious shortcomings with this case, I came to tell you something I think you deserve to know."

I sipped my drink and said, "Well, at least you are willing to *admit* you fucked up. So, what is it you want to tell me?"

Crow said, "I just wanted you to know, if it hadn't been for you giving me that information, this case might have gone cold. At least for a long time, anyway. I just wanted to say thank you."

I said, "Well, I appreciate the sentiment, but it doesn't change the fact that my interference in the case helped cause her death. She trusted me, and I betrayed that trust, and now she is *dead*."

Crow said, "Welcome to *my* world, Polanski. I have felt what you're feeling right now more times than I can count, and it never gets easier."

I said, "Well, I pity you on that aspect, but that's it. You're still an asshole."

Crow said, "I can be, yes. But I solve my cases and *move on*. You need to the same thing, before it eats you up inside like a cancer."

Sipping my drink again, I said, "My whole *life* had been a cancer, Crow. Now, is there anything else you have to say? I'm busy getting drunk, if you haven't noticed."

As he turned to walk away, all Crow had to say was, "Goodbye, Polanski, and good luck."

"Go screw yourself," I said, and walked inside, to my own little world, where I may be drunk most of the time but still feel safe regardless.

And so it goes.

TWENTY TWO

I had gone on another one of my binges, this one lasting around four days.

The blackouts, the nightmares.

Most of the nightmares were about Patty.

Watching her pull the trigger.

Watching helplessly as she gulps down a handful of pain pills and chases it with liquor and then places the barrel of the .22 against her pretty face, and pulls the trigger, her brains exiting the back of her head in a red mist, as she looks at me and says, *You betrayed me, and now look at me. I said, LOOK AT ME.*

I *do* look, and wake up screaming.

#

And so it goes.

But, like Crow said, *Move on before it eats you up like a cancer.*

For once, maybe he was right.

So, I moved on.

#

The next day, after a delicious breakfast of beer and Cheerios, I had decided to pass on any computer work and spend some time outside in the sunshine.

I hadn't been tending to Missy's gravesite lately, either, and that sweet little kitty deserved better.

I went out front, picked a small handful of flowers from the garden, and went out back to spruce up her grave a little bit.

After weeding the grave, I placed the fresh flowers on her grave, and sat chatting with her for a while.

Sone people might consider it odd to sit by an animal's grave and speak to them, but to a real pet lover like myself, it's no more strange than a human being visiting a loved one's grave and speaking to them.

Besides, if anyone thinks I'm odd for doing so, they can kiss my ass.

#

I had just finished our little chat, and was sitting at the picnic table sipping a beer, when I heard the sound of a cat nearby, meowing so sadly.

I looked up to see a tiny, scrawny little female cat, her little green eyes encrusted with dried up tears and her fur filthy and bug ridden.

I could tell she had been beautiful at one time, with thick black fur that shined like blue steel in the sunlight, and big, emerald green eyes.

But that was long ago and far away for this little girl; like so many other beings on this Earth, she had been forgotten and left to fend for herself, alone and hungry and thirsty.

I reached down and picked her up, cradling her in my arms, stroking her fur and telling her it was going to be alright.

It was at that very moment, I began to wonder if she was *meant* to be here, if it wasn't Missy – and God – who had intervened, telling me to adopt this little angel.

So I did.

I carried her inside, and found some old canned cat food left over from Missy's stash, opened a can of tuna platter, and watched as the kitten devoured it so fast you would have thought she hadn't eaten in weeks.

After gobbling up the cat food, and drinking about half of a bowl of ice water, I'd brushed her fur out with flea power, and given her a bath in the kitchen sink.

Afterward, I had fluffed her with a towel and brushed her fur out again, restoring her natural beauty.

And what a beautiful – and sweet – cat she was.

As we sat on the couch together that night, me drinking beer and watching *Forensic Files* and her laying next to me, purring up a storm and playing with a catnip mouse, I had realized I hadn't thought of a name for my new roommate.

It hadn't taken long to think of one.

The name I came up with, I thought was very befitting under the circumstances.

I named her Patty.

David Boyer is a Christian, a multi-genre writer, a true crime buff, and the author of several coming of age novellas, numerous horror and scifi stories, as well as the author of numerous essays including the subjects of government corruption, Christianity, bullying, and cyber-stalking.

He lives in Vincennes, Indiana, with his cat, Holly Jean, who now serves as his copy editor by jumping on the computer keyboard when he's not looking.

Books: {Non-fiction}
True crime:
Small Town Murder: True Crime Stories From Knox County, Indiana
Murder In the Hoosier Heartland: Infamous Indiana Murderers & Fledgling Serial Killers
Murder & Mayhem In the Hoosier Heartland: Mysterious Disappearances & Bizarre Murders In Indiana
The Blitz: A Rape Victim's Story
Vanished In Vincennes: the Mysterious Disappearance and Death Of Dolores Oliver
47 Years of Hell: The Dolores Oliver Murder: Still Unsolved
Small Town Murder In Knox County, Indiana: Hate Crimes, Witch Hunts, and A Definitive List of Indiana Serial Killers
The Guy In The Blue Shirt

Non-fiction: {paranormal, bio & memoir}
Haunted Heartland: Haunted Hoosiers Tell Their Ghost Stories
Strange Happenings In the Hoosier Heartland
I Remember When, In Vincennes...Volume 1
Growing Up In Vincennes – Volumes 2 – 5
The Time of Our Lives: Growing Up Cool In Vincennes, Indiana

Essays:
Bullying: the Road to Recovery and Forgiveness
Privacy In the Age of the Internet: How Sexting and Sharing Private Photos Can lead To Cyber-Stalking
Once An Alcoholic, Always An Alcoholic? The Cold Hard Truth

About Our Addictions
Travesties of Jutice: Flaws In Our Legal System That Imprison the Innocent
Will the REAL Christian Please Stand Up?
Racism in the 21st Century: ALL Lives Matter
Conflicted Souls: How the Man In Black Saved My Life
Crossing the Rainbow Bridge: Saying Goodbye To Our Beloved Pets

Books: {Fiction}
Mystery, Indiana
Human Sawdust

Stories: {Long fiction, novellas}
Mystery, Indiana
The Mind of Luther Biggs
LUTHER
Jenny
Lester Talbot and His Magic Eye
Beautiful Ghosts
Pretty Flamingo
Jack and Norma Jean
The Things We Leave Behind – Volumes 1 – 3
Ghosts of Summer
Gardens
Claustrophobia
The Cemetery Artist
Brain Pie
Beast
The Jailhouse Movie Star
Easy Pickings
The Dominant Thumb
Joyride
The Maverick
Freak
Grandma's Gooseberry Pie
Dancing With the King
Always In My Heart

Other recent book releases by David Boyer
{Now available on Lulu.com}

Dolores Oliver, fondly nick-named 'Lert' by her friends as a term of endearment, was out an out-going and friendly woman who was well liked by all who knew her.

Yet, on September 7, 1974, while on a visit to a local bar to chat with friends, she simply vanished without a trace. Foul play was immediately suspected by her family, who knew in their hearts that they could think of absolutely no one who would want to do her any harm.

Yet her lifeless body was found at the end of October in a bean field by a farmer in Illinois. Lawrence County coroner Dale Nichols was able to make a positive ID through dental records and a ring Mrs Oliver was wearing.

Who would have done such a thing, and why? Hopefully, VANISHED IN VINCENNES will help to finally solve one of the oldest cold cases in Indiana, and bring her family some closure they have sought for so long.

I

Remember
When, In
Vincennes...

Hometown Stories From
Vincennes, Indiana - Volume 1

David Boyer

Unfortunately, even small towns – Vincennes included – eventually change, sometimes for the better, and other times, not so much. It's the natural order of things.

Trees grow old and fall. Sidewalks split and crack and are replaced for public safety's sake. Old houses – and all the memories associated with them – are demolished and replaced with parking lots or duplexes. Even historical landmarks, Mother Nature and Father Time having taken their toll, sadly, vanish – except for our own pictures and memories of them.

Luckily for Vincennes residents, local historian Norbert Brown has created a Facebook group page entitled, *Vincennes Remember When*, to help all of us keep our fond memories intact, and to reminisce and enjoy them 24-7.

It was his infinite wisdom of our local history and group page that was the inspiration for this book – and the stories within. Some of these stories may elicit a tear, some laughter.

Some may remind you of an old friend you haven't seen since high school – or, sadly, one that has passed in recent years. Some may remind you of your childhood, your teenage years – or having to bid them farewell, in order to move on to bigger and better things; marriage, children, grandchildren, and a lifetime of wonderful memories that only a tight-knit, loving family can provide.

It is my sincere belief that there will be a story for *everybody* within these pages, regardless of whether you may be a Vincennes history buff or not.

As of 2015, it is believed that there are at least 200 serial killers active in the United States at any given time.

33 of them were from Indiana.

Nobody in their own home town would have wanted to imagine a fledgling {or full fledged} serial killer lurking about, searching for his next victim. Or imagine one being their next door neighbor or the relative of a friend or even attending the local college.

Yet, since the early 1970s, Vincennes, Indiana, Knox County, and Indiana in general has had it's share of cold blooded murder.

It's really sad – as well as terrifying – to even imagine all these brutal, cold blooded murders have taken place in small town communities, where, at one time, we could all trust just about everyone we met at least to the extent they'd do us no harm; a time when could leave our doors unlocked at night or a window open for a cool breeze or not have to worry about where our children were – or if they'd ever come home again.

In SMALL TOWN MURDER, we will be examining local cases, old cases, more recent cases, and the aftermath it leaves behind for the victim's families – as well as taking an in-depth look into a deep, dark, world none of us would ever want to see – but has been here all along, and, most likely, always will be.

Bonus:
Excerpts from the book
The Ghosts In My Head
A Chuck Polanski Novel
By David Boyer

ONE

The terrible secret of my writing is that I don't have the imagination I used to have. I need to go to a place, soak in its atmosphere, its nuance, and let it speak to me. I'm sitting in a rear corner booth in Bud's tavern, a known haunt for the walking wounded when they are looking for love in all the wrong places Under the crimson glare of the bar's lights, I stare out at a sea of empty lives.

Men and women searching for the momentary distraction of drunken comradery to numb themselves from the pain of their own reality. The décor reeks of a pervasive hopelessness that has settled even into the Formica tables; an air of desperation as thick as the spent Scotch fumes from the nearby table.

Believe it or not, here I find inspiration.

What we believe, why we believe –from nihilistic to religious–are a part of us and thus a part of our writing. We all have stories, mine is no better than anyone else's, all of us leading broken lives to one degree or another in this drama of life. And I find inspiration writing about redemption, about wringing hope from hopelessness. I find solace in writing stories about those living on the fringe of society, yet not quite ever teetering over the edge of oblivion. I've been there, done that, so I'm most definitely writing what I know.

Thus the life of a drunk.

#

There is no such thing as an alcoholic.

If you're a drunk, you're a drunk.

Might as well not try to sugarcoat a turd.

It always kills me to hear someone refer to a drunk as a "recovering alcoholic." Once the demon alcohol digs it's claws into you, you *belong* to it.

You always crave it, desire it, like you would a long lost lover who has vanished like a wisp of smoke in a high wind.

You dream about it, and wake up each morning in love with it.

It is your constant companion, your lover, your confidant. Your one and only *real* friend, that you can always count on to be there when you need it.

And it's the one and only thing that can silence the ghosts in my head.

TWO

The ghosts in my head.

Now, bear in mind, ghosts don't necessarily have to be disembodied souls.

A ghost can be a mere memory of someone or something that you used to be so close to. Like a pair of old, gold cufflinks, an old, moth eaten suit hanging in a closet, or an old photograph of a deceased loved one.

The ghost in my head is the demon alcohol, always there to haunt me, to remind me I belong to it, and I better be faithful and grateful for what it has so lovingly bestowed upon me.

So I write.

#

Writing has become my primary outlet for venting my frustrations, to create so many different worlds in which I am happy again, and free.

Free from my own sad memories of who I *used* to be, and wish I was again, but then I'd have to give up my best friend and I could never do that.

I don't want to seem ungrateful, you know.

I write because I feel I need to, to still the voices in my head. Because something in the core of my being crawls up and takes hold of me to move pen to paper.

To think, as I sit here drumming my fingers along this table waiting for inspiration to hit me, all I need is a pad and a pen and a place for something mystical and profound, yet simple and ordinary, to happen. To think, as I sit staring into the lonely eyes of strangers, I used to be just like them, and they are still just like I used to be. We are all connected in the grand scheme of things; we are all only human.

Or, at least I *used* to be human, anyway.

I'm not sure what I am anymore, but I'm also quite sure that I will figure it out – as long as I continue to write.

I have to silence those nasty little ghosts somehow, you know?

So...I write.

THREE

I guess you don't have to be a great writer, though, to 'write what you know,' so here I am again, sitting amongst the walking wounded and feeling right at home. Sometimes, exploring the darker side of humanity has its advantages – from a distance.

But believe it or not, even a full fledged, dedicated drunk like yours truly can only take so much drunken comradery with my fellow drunks before I need a much deserved break from it all.

Misery loves company, and I'm already miserable enough as it is.

So...I go home to my dark, dismal little room and I write.

But, not before I indulge in a little of "the hair of the dog that bit me."

I don't want to seem unfaithful, you know.

#

First I drink, then I write.

I must stick to my *normal* schedule – or whatever might *pass* for normal these days.

I have my daily schedule down to a science:

Six am – crawl out of bed, light a cigarette, knock back a couple of beers.

Seven am – stagger into the shower, let the hot water flow over my body, opening my pores and sweating out all of the cheap hooch I'd ingested the night before.

Seven thirty am – shave, dress, and down another beer or two.

Eight am – Walk outside, listen to the birdies sing and the crickets chirp and watch the sun come up over the horizon, signaling the beginning of another fine day in the life of a hopeless drunk.

Eight thirty am – Open my new bottle of bourbon, pour a double shot, down it, pour another, then sit down at my ancient laptop and begin working on yet another Pulitzer Prize worthy pile of shit that nobody will ever read, but might bring in a few extra bucks down the road I can use to buy some cheap wine.

In my shoes, you have to remain optimistic, you know?

#

As Kurt Vonnegut once said, *And so it goes.*

So it goes for me again today, as I sit writing my newest novel, *The Ghosts In My Head.*

Fair warning, my friends; this book may not be for the faint of heart.

With that being said, let us continue.

FOUR

As we move forward, let me make it all too clear to any aspiring writers, don't think you are going to become rich and famous anytime soon.

I don't care if you have the literary promise of Salinger and Steinbeck, if you don't have a *very good* manuscript in hand – and the luck of the Irish on your side, you may be very disappointed.

I, myself, gave up long ago on the idea of penning the next great American novel, and instead stuck to what I know best; writing what I *feel*.

Writing what you *know*.

Sometimes, the truth really is stranger than fiction – and much more informative and entertaining.

Take for example, writing about the life and times of your average drunkard.

#

Your average drunk was just like anybody else at one time. Just your regular Joe muddling through life as best he can, working a dead end job and going home in the evenings to a luke warm beer and TV dinners.

He slowly but surely becomes disillusioned by it all until he begins coming home each night to skip dinner and drink his meals instead.

He keeps on drinking and drinking and drinking, until he loses his job, then his family, and then his home.

He ends up on the street, an empty, former shell of himself, eating day old donuts out of dumpsters and sleeping in the park, and spends the rest of his day begging for chump change so he can buy another bottle of MD 20-20 or Thunderbird.

By that time, he is nothing more than a *ghost* of his former self, drifting through the crowded streets almost totally unnoticed by the rest of society, just another lost soul in a sea of empty lives.

Like I said, I write what I *know*.

FIVE

Back to the subject of writing, I do have a major source of inspiration on my side.

My cat, Missy.

It was March of 2022, almost 14 months since my cat, Toby, had passed away from sickness and old age.

I had never really gotten used to the idea of his passing, and I was still very lonely and bored, still missing him, and as all pet lovers know, there is nothing to really fill that void left behind by a beloved pet.

I carried on with my daily routine, working on my computer, TV, housework, etc., but absolutely *nothing* could keep my mind off how miserable I was deep down inside.

Then one day in early March of that year, I had made the decision that all true fur baby lovers make eventually; it was time to look for another kitty cat.

As it turned out, I had most definitely made the right decision.

#

When I arrived at the animal shelter, I was greeted by tons of kitty cats, most of them running to greet me with open paws and sweet little meows.

If you are a true cat lover like me, then you will already know what was going through my mind; I wanted to take ALL of them home.

But as I made my way through the room, practically tripping over kitty cats, my eyes were suddenly fixed on a cage in the corner of the room, away from the other cages. Inside was a tiny, dark tabby female cat, laying in the cage with her front paws laid out before her, and her tiny little head nestled between those paws, looking as sad and lonely as a cat had a right to do.

Her big green eyes fixed on mine, too, but a second later she was closing her eyes and turning over, away from my line of sight, as though she was already giving up, in fear of yet another rejection, and would rather be asleep than to face another heartache.

I asked the lady that worked there about the kitty's background, and the story she told me would break even the coldest of hearts; she had been picked up as an unhealthy stray, and apparently the runt of her litter.

Since she'd been a resident of the shelter, she had been picked on by larger cats, had to fight for food unless it was placed in her cage, and in general, been miserable for most of her stay there so far.

As I listened to her sad story, I knew that she was the one I would take home that day. After all, we we had so much in common, too.

She needed me as much as I needed her, so I took her home to become part of the family.

Her *forever* home.

If I had my way, everyone would have a cat. Cats are magnificent creatures, in every way.

All I have to do to feel better these days is just *look* at my cat, watch her rolling around in the floor playing with her catnip toys and looking up at me with her big, green, intelligent eyes, and my stone cold heart melts, even if only briefly.

If I had my way, I would have fifty cats in my house, because I sincerely believe that the more cats you have around you, the longer you will live.

They are bright, life giving saviors, their inner light and being prolonging your own.

Yeah...I know.

You are thinking, how could a lazy, drunken bum of a failed writer have such a big heart?

Well, let me tell you, most of the drunks I've met in my lifetime had the biggest hearts of all. Why is it, you think, that their heart was broken so easily, sending them spiralling down into a state of such hopelessness?

A drunk wears their heart on their sleeve, and, more often than not, and that is their curse.

They are no harm to anyone – other than themselves. But that's their downfall; they haven't learned to love *themselves* again.

Just a thought.